Anyone can
Anyone can be a millionaire!

A guide to turning your business
idea into a reality

Dean Dunham

Dean Dunham Publishing
Unit 4, York Farm Business Park,
Watling Street East,
Towcester,
Northants,
NN12 8TU

0845 0066 276
www.dunhamcompanies.co.uk

Copyright © Dean Dunham 2007

ISBN: 978-0-9556191-0-6

Anyone can be a successful entrepreneur if they are determined and the fact that you are reading this book already demonstrates a degree of determination. That's a great start!

I want to start with a valuable piece of advice – believe in yourself. To succeed as an entrepreneur, you need to have a 'can do' attitude. If you do not believe in yourself, it will show and with this being the case, you will never be able to convince those who matter (i.e.: your family, bank, investors, customers) to believe in you and support you.

I would like to dedicate this book to those who have believed in me, in particular my family (particularly my business and personal partner Jo) Martin Cadman of HSBC and all those who have worked with me. Without these people I would not be where I am today. Thank you.

Welcome to the d club...

I am delighted that you have chosen to buy my book. I've worked really hard to make this book useful to potential entrepreneurs and I really hope that it assists you in your quest.

As you will now be aware, as a purchaser of this book you are entitled to a 10% discount with two of my companies - **Dunham Solicitors LLP** (which will be useful for you when you need to buy or lease premises, employment contracts, commercial agreements or general commercial law advice) and **Dunham Media** (which can help you with all design matters including your branding and with the design and development of your website).

Take advantage of these discounts as these are all services which you will need for your start-up company.

In addition to the above, you are also entitled to a 12 month membership of *deandunham.com*. Within the site you will see that there is a 'member's area' where you can email myself and my team questions. We will then assist you via email where we can.

To activate the above benefits, please send your receipt for the purchase of this book to:

Dunham Book Membership Team
12 Walker Avenue
Stratford Office Village
Wolverton Mill
Milton Keynes
MK12 5TW

Once this has been received you will be emailed a user name and password so that you can access the 'member section' of *dean**dunham**.com* and, in addition, email you a discount reference so that you can take advantage of the aforementioned discount schemes.

Scope of book

Firstly, when reading this book, it is important to keep in mind what the subject matter of the book is. My aim has been to give you vital information and advice on the fundamental basics of starting a business and setting solid groundworks for a successful venture.

There are obviously parts of the book where I touch on subjects that are really outside of its scope (i.e.: accounting matters, employment law etc). On these subjects you should either consult with a professional advisor, a specialised book on the relevant subject matter or email my 'help' facility if you want to know more.

Idea behind book

The basic idea behind this book is to take your business idea (which will be for a service or product) and create a successful business. Accordingly, I will take you through all of the steps and thought processes that you need to go through between coming up with your idea and launching it as a business.

With this being the case, this book really does need to be read in the order that it appears on the first occasion that you read it.

Tips

Throughout the book you will see grey boxes with tips in. These are my tips designed to help you and come from my personal experiences.

Definitions

I have tried to keep the language in this book 'plain English'. However, in some cases, this is impossible so you may find certain words that are unfamiliar to you. Accordingly, where this is the case, you will find red definitions boxes where the meanings of the words are explained.

Contents

YOUR BUSINESS IDEA

'believe in
yourself!'

By this stage you have decided that you do not want to work for someone else for the rest of your life, this won't make you rich. You will have either already made the leap of faith and started your own venture or have definite plans to take such a step. Guess what? You're an entrepreneur!

Every new venture should be well thought out before you commit your time and resources to it.

During your analysis of the idea you should consider the following:

- Is your idea unique or has it been done before?
- Who is your competition?
- Is there a need for the service or product?
- How much will it cost to start the business?
- Will you need to borrow cash to start the business?
- What equipment will you need to start the business?
- What will you call the business?
- Will you be a sole trader, partnership or limited company?
- Do you need staff?
- Where will you trade from?
- How much money do you need to live on?
- Are there any specific legal requirements?

This book will touch on all of these matters.

Protecting your idea

Before you start telling the world about your idea you need to make sure that it is legally protected. One thing you can be sure of, if your idea is generally good, it will be copied!

A detailed analysis of methods for protecting your idea is outside the scope of this book, however you should consider the following:

1. If your idea is a 'product' you should consider making an application to register a patent. Before making an application, you will need to carry out a search at the UK Patent Office (www.patent.gov.uk) to make sure that no other similar patents have been filed.

    Obtaining a patent can be very expensive and time consuming. Also, it is advisable to use the services of a patent agent which obviously attracts additional costs. However, if your application is successful, it will give you a great deal of protection for your idea and it will therefore follow that the idea will be more attractive to investors, banks and potential purchasers of your business later on.

2. If you do not have the funds available to pursue a patent application, you could document your idea and post it to yourself by 'Special Delivery'. When you receive the document leave the envelope sealed. This will then give you a clear record of the date that you came up with the idea. This may help you if a dispute arises in the future with a third party.

3. You can protect certain works under the law of copyright by inserting the © symbol, the name of the copyright owner and the year of publication on documents. See *www.patent.gov.uk* for more information.

4. You can protect a 'design' (i.e. overall appearance such as colour, texture, shape and material by one of the following methods:

    *   Unregistered design right
    *   Registering the design
    *   Copyright protection

    See *www.patent.gov.uk* for more information.

Non-Disclosure Agreement

When discussing or disclosing your idea to anyone it is advisable to get them to sign a non-disclosure agreement. This will prohibit them from stealing the idea for themselves or disclosing it to a third party.

The content of this book really is about forming a business from your business idea. However, it is worth quickly noting what the alternative routes are if you do not want to do this but still want to exploit the idea.

1. **Selling the idea**

   You could approach an individual or company who you think would like to buy the idea and sell it. If you do this, remember the contents earlier on in this chapter, "Protecting your idea". Also, if you take this route you will obviously make far less money out of the idea.

2. Licence the idea

This is similar to the above but instead of actually 'selling' the idea you can grant a licence for it to be used in return for receiving a licence fee.

3. Collaboration/Joint venture

This basically means that you get somebody else involved in running the business with you.

FORMING YOUR BUSINESS

'it will be worth it in the end'

Trading Style

You have your business idea and, after giving it a great deal of thought, you believe that it is worth pursuing. You now need to decide what style you will run the business under. Your options are as follows:

- Sole trader
- Partnership
- Limited Company
- Limited Liability Partnership
- Public Limited Company

It is important that you choose the correct trading style for your business. In deciding you should consider the following:

Sole Trader

This means that you are trading under your name (or a made up name) effectively on your own and that you are not any of the other trading styles listed above.

Advantages:
- Simplest way to set up a business
- Easiest way to keep records and accounts

Disadvantage:
- You will be 'personally' liable for everything that the business does and all debts etc.

Partnership

This is where two or more people are in business together as self-employed people.

Advantages:
- Easy to set up and run
- All risks and costs are shared between the partners

Disadvantages:
- As with a Sole Trader, each partner is personally liable for everything that the business does and all debts etc.
- Potential for partners to disagree and fall out on various matters.

Limited Liability Partnership

This is a cross between a Partnership and a Limited Company and therefore shares similarities to both. Put simply, it is a Limited Company with 'partners' instead of shareholders.

Advantages:
- The liability of the partners is 'limited'
- Risks, costs and responsibilities are shared.

Disadvantage:
- More costly and complex to set up than a partnership.

Limited Company

This is the most common form of trading style. Under this set-up the owners of the business are known as 'shareholders'.

Advantages:
- The company is its 'own entity', therefore meaning that the shareholders are not responsible for all of the company's actions
- The maximum extent of the shareholders' liability financially is the amount that they have invested.

Disadvantage:
- Significant legal obligations - such as keeping records at Companies House updated.

Public Limited Company

This means that the company is publicly trading on a stock exchange and therefore that the public can buy and sell shares in the company.

Advantages:
- Can sound prestigious
- Good way to raise money

Disadvantage:
- Very complex and expensive to run

To me there are ultimately 2 main considerations when deciding which style to use, namely:

1. **Tax** – you should speak to an accountant as to which style is best for you from a tax aspect; and

2. **Market perception** – you need to know your customers. Some people may prefer to deal with a Limited Company as opposed to a sole trader, as there is a perception that a sole trader is small. However, with some businesses small is beautiful so don't make a generalisation.

If you're still not sure which style to trade under log on to *'help me'* on **deandunham.com** and give me a description of your particular circumstances.

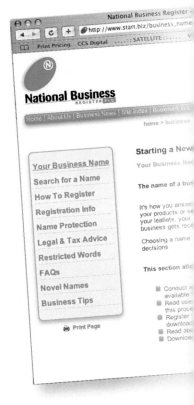

Business Name

You have a great business idea and you have decided your trading style. You now need a name. I'm a great believer in brainstorming using flow charts. This is a perfect example of when to use this. Think of every name that comes to mind and get it on to paper. Once you have done this look at which ones stand out. Get a second and third opinion on this as well. This will then help you to eliminate those that do not fit.

Once you have your shortlist you need to consider the following points:

1.   Are there any other companies with the same name? – a good starting point in researching this is to look on Companies House website ***www.companieshouse. co.uk.*** This is a free service. You can also look on The National Business Register at ***www.anewbusiness.co.uk.***

    You may find that a company previously used your name but that it has now been dissolved. If this is the case, my advice would be not to use the name.

2. **Legal constraints** – you will need to make sure that your business name does not include the words 'plc', 'limited' or the equivalent and does not contain sensitive words or expressions (i.e. a word or expression that would suggest a special status for your business such as *'Council'* or *'Chartered'*).

3. **Branding** – see chapter 6.

Company Formation

A limited company (LTD), limited liability company (LLP) and a public limited company (PLC) are all entities in their own right. This means that they need to be 'formed'. On the other hand a sole trader and partnership are not their own entities as a sole trader's entity is the actual person behind it and a partnership's entity is that of the partners.

Limited Company

There are 2 ways of forming a limited company, namely:

1. **Buy an off-shelf company**; or
2. **Incorporate the company yourself**

OFF-SHELF – You can acquire an off-shelf company from incorporation agents, solicitors and accountants. These generally cost between £50-£100. For this they will sell you a 'ready made' Limited Company which simply needs a change of name and change of shareholders and officers (i.e.: directors and secretary).

SELF INCORPORATION – You can incorporate a Limited Company yourself by completing various Companies House forms. These can be obtained from Companies House website for free, *www.companieshouse.co.uk*.

You will need to complete the following:

* Form 10
* Form 12

Your Form 12 will need to be sworn in front of a solicitor.

In addition to the above you will also need to have a set of Articles of Association and Memorandum of Association. You can obtain precedents of these from the member's section of *deandunham.com*.

Once you have all of the above, you will need to send everything to Companies House along with a cheque for the incorporation fee. You will find details of the incorporation fee on Companies House website. You should therefore send your Form 10, Form 12, Articles of Association, Memorandum of Association and cheque for the incorporation fee to:

Registrar of Companies
Companies House
Crown Way, Maindy, Cardiff, CF14 3UZ

You should receive a certificate of incorporation from Companies House within 14 days. This will have your company number which should be displayed on all of your stationery (see chapter 3).

Limited Liability Partnership

The process for incorporating a Limited Liability Partnership is the same as with a Limited Company except that you will need to complete a Form LLP2 instead of Forms 10 and 12 as mentioned above. This can be obtained from Companies House website.

SPECIFIC LEGAL REQUIREMENTS

Different laws apply to different types of companies. Accordingly, you need to ascertain whether your particular business type has any specific laws or regulations that it must follow.

For example, the following businesses are governed by specific laws and regulations:

Handy Tips

To register for VAT look on www.hmrc.gov.uk

Children's Day Nursery
OFSTED/ Children's Act 1985

Law Firm
Law Society/ Solicitors Act 1984

Restaurant
Food Safety Laws

In addition to the above, you should consider the following:

Value Added Tax (VAT)

You would have noticed on numerous occasions when you have purchased something that the price has been stipulated as a certain price 'plus VAT'. This particularly applies to a business as most of your suppliers will charge you VAT.

Any business (except those which are exempt) can register for VAT. If a business is registered, it means that on the one hand it must add VAT to all of its sales but on the other hand it can claim back all VAT that it pays to its suppliers.

Example:

X Limited is registered for VAT. In January it spends £1175 on supplies (i.e.: stationery etc). VAT is charged at 17.5% therefore meaning that £175 of the above represents VAT.

In the same month X Limited (which is a cleaning service) receives £5875 in sales. £875 of this represents VAT at 17.5% that X Limited has charged to its customers.

Accordingly, When X Limited accounts to the VAT office it will have to pay them the sum of £700 (i.e.: the amount of VAT that it has charged its customers less the amount of VAT that it has paid to its suppliers).

Whilst you will initially have a choice whether or not to register for VAT, if your turnover exceeds a certain amount (see the VAT website for current amount) you will have to register by law.

Stationery

1. If your business is registered at Companies House (therefore meaning that you are a Limited Company, Limited Liability Partnership or Public Limited Company) you will need to display the following on your company stationery:

- The company name (exactly as it appears at Companies House
- The company's registered office address
- The country in which the company is registered (i.e. England & Wales or Scotland)
- The company number allocated by Companies House
- The VAT number (if applicable)

2. If you are a partnership or sole trader, you will need to display the following:

- The business trading name
- The names of partners/sole trader
- The VAT number (if applicable)

START-UP COSTS

'add 10% to all costs'

Nearly all new entrepreneurs either underestimate the cost of starting up a business or simply fail to give this any consideration!

It is obviously vitally important that your business does not run out of money. The key to this is maintaining good cash flow forecasts. To get this started on the right foot you obviously need to have a good grasp of how much money you will have to spend to get your business started.

Definition

Cash Flow Forecast:

The forecast of monies to be spent and received.

Log on to the member's section on **deandunham**.com *for samples.*

Obviously your start-up costs will vary depending upon what type of business you are starting. However, the following is an example list for a typical company. You can use this as a template for your list.

ITEM	COST	MY TIPS
Computers		You will see many cheap computer deals being offered by computer shops and indeed by manufacturers. Whilst these sound like great deals, be careful, as often they do not actually include the relevant software that you need. Software in some cases can more expensive than the hardware! Do not be tempted into buying a cheap used computer. Computer technology these days evolves rapidly and you will probably find that you quickly have to replace the computer, thus costing you more than you would have spent if you had bought new in the first place.
Printers		If you do not need to print in colour buy a black and white printer. These are not only cheaper to buy, but also far cheaper to run.
Desks		
Chairs		

ITEM	COST	MY TIPS
Telephones		
Stationery		Buy an initial 'stationery pack' which will include an initial supply of letterheads, compliments slips and business cards.
		As I have stressed elsewhere in this book, image is really important to a business, especially a new business trying to find its way. Accordingly, do not cut corners with stationery.
Fax machine		Consider if you need this as it may not be essential to your business. If you want the ability to receive faxes but do not need to send them consider using efax. See *www.efax.co.uk*
Companies House incorporation fee		

Brand design, your company website (see Chapter 6), initial advertising and initial stock (if applicable) costs also need to be considered.

Obviously there may be many other items but this list will get you started.

RESEARCH YOUR MARKET

'be inspired
by your
competition'

Before an army goes into battle it ascertains as much information as possible about the enemy and therefore carefully plans its attack. Knowing what the enemy has to offer is vital to knowing how to exploit its weaknesses.

Going into business is no different to this. It is simply not enough to have a great business idea. You need to know:

- who your competition is
- what they offer
- how good they are
- what they charge
- whether your service or product is better

There are a number of ways to find out who your competition is. Some of these are:

1. **Yellow Pages** – remember that the Yellow Pages is in 'regions'. Accordingly, if you are looking to provide a service or sell a product 'nationally' this may not be the best source for information.

2. **Yell.com** – like the Yellow Pages this is set in regions.

3. **Google search** – simply go to www.google.co.uk and then enter the service or product that applies to you (i.e.: children's day nurseries). You could also use a different search engine, such as MSN, ask etc..

4. **Local Business Directories**

5. **Phone book**

What are you looking for?

When looking at the competition there are some core things that you should look out for:

- Branding – what is their brand like? Do they stand out? Do they look good? etc. Once you have ascertained this you need to make sure that your branding is better. As I have said on numerous occasions throughout this book, this is really important. Branding is everything and if your competition has a better brand it is not a good start.

- Price – how much does the competition charge? What do their charges include? How does this compare to your charges? There are many theories on how a 'start-up' business should charge. If you read some of the business books written by academics you will see phrases such as 'killer pricing' (i.e.: undercutting the competition) and 'creating a high price point' (i.e.: being more expensive than the competition so that you create a perception that you have a better service or product.) Total nonsense!! The people who come up with these ideas are simply academics who have no perception of the real world.

Ok, so you are now thinking that I am mad: How can he say that 'undercutting' our competition on price is a bad idea? Surely it will lead to an inflow of business and accordingly will leave the competition suffering. I absolutely agree. However, whilst it will seem good in the short term it will not help your business long-term. In this respect you should be aware that 90% of 'start-up' companies fail in their first year and this is because they deploy short sighted tactics like this.

If you set your prices low it will be extremely difficult for you to get them back to where they should be, as your customers' price expectations would have been set.

On the converse setting your prices higher than the competition is simply business suicide. The only exception to this is if you genuinely have a product or service that is far superior to that of the competition and therefore is worth more.

Generally speaking you should set your prices at the same level as the competition.

- **What do they actually offer?**

- **What are their strengths?**

- What are their weaknesses?

- What marketing do they do?
  – Where do they advertise?
  Who are they aiming at? Also,
  what marketing materials do
  they have (brochures, website
  etc..) Telephone and pretend to
  be a potential customer so that
  you can hear their sales pitch
  and see what they send out as
  part of their pitch.

When you have concluded your
research you need to revisit your
business idea and marketing
plan. You must then ask yourself
whether you still think that the
idea is viable, bearing in mind the
competition and if so whether your
marketing plan is strong enough to
outwit your competition.

Handy Tips

*Be inspired by
the competition,
rather than
getting worried
about what they
are offering,
enjoy the
challenge of
being better than
them.*

Handy Tips

*Carry out market
research on your
competition at
least once every
six months!*

BRANDING

'branding is important; make sure you get this right!'

I cannot stress enough how important branding is. I have always taken branding seriously with my companies and believe that this has played a big part in my success.

Just to clarify, this includes anything that carries your logo, such as;

- Your letterheads
- Your website
- Your business cards
- Your brochures

Your branding via the above will probably be the first perception people will have of your company and for this reason it is vitally important. If your branding is weak your company will not look good. You can also use branding to tell the outside world what sort of company you are. For example, if you want the company to be seen as a 'young, modern and dynamic' business your branding should reflect this.

I really want to make sure that you fully understand why I say branding is so important.

Have a look at illustration 1 below. This is a self- made logo. What does it say to you about the company? To me it says:

- Small
- Unprofessional
- Home made
- Old fashioned
- Cheap
- Shoestring

Now look at illustration 2. What does this say? To me it says:

- Professional
- Could be big or small but doesn't matter
- Modern
- Dynamic
- Stylish

Use the services of a graphic designer to design your logo and stationery and get your stationery professionally printed.

Investing into your brand is investing into your company's reputation!

You should also consider the following points with your designer:

- **Colours of the brand** – the more colours you use the more expensive it will be to run adverts in papers/magazines etc. and the more expensive it will be to apply your branding to products.

- **What your logo will be applied to** – does the size and complexity matter?

Handy Tips

Don't:

☐ *Design your own logo (unless you're a designer)*

☐ *Design and print your own letterheads*

☐ *Scrimp on your budget for brand design*

Definition

Branding:

The process by which the true character and purpose of the company or organisation is communicated.

In chapter 11 I will talk further about the importance of your branding when talking to your bank.

Your Website

We now live in an 'internet' world with most people and nearly every company having internet access. It therefore follows that most people look at a company's website before using their services or buying from them.

Your website is therefore really important and, like your brand, it will tell many of your potential customers who you are and what your company is all about. To illustrate this imagine that you want to buy a soldering iron online and you find the two websites below.

You need the best soldering iron available and need to get support quickly if anything goes wrong. Which one would you buy from?

Hopefully you decided that you would want to buy from site 2. If you didn't, please email with your reasons why as I would be fascinated to hear them.

Ok, assuming that like me you chose site 2, lets just clarify why. For me, site 1 fails for the following reasons:

- It looks homemade
- It does not give me confidence to buy online
- It does not jump out and say that this is a professional company which will look after me as a customer

In contrast site 2:

- Looks professional
- Gives me confidence
- Makes me feel that I will be looked after

So you can see how important a good website is and what it can do for your image and indeed sales. I will talk more about selling via your website in chapter 12.

Make sure that your site is easy to use and understand. Ask friends to look at the site and critique it for you.

Handy Tips

Websites do not necessarily have to cost the earth. If your budget is tight you are better to have a small but very professional looking site as opposed to a large mediocre site. Web designers tend to cost a site depending on how many pages it has.

Make sure that the site is
consistent with the rest
of your branding and
accordingly that it portrays
the correct image.

Handy Tips

*Check the site
very carefully for
typos*

EMPLOYING STAFF

'know your limitations'

All good entrepreneurs know their limitations and know when to ask for help. If you don't know something, ask! Remember no-one 'knows it all' and those who have that mentality are sure to fail.

During the build up of my group of companies, I have surrounded myself with some exceptional people, who are knowledgeable in areas where I am not an expert. Employment law is a minefield as it changes constantly. Accordingly, I have asked Fiona Hewitt, an employment lawyer at my law firm, Dunham Solicitors LLP, to write this chapter.

Be careful who you employ!

You must always make sure that the person you are intending to employ is allowed to work here. Employing someone who is not entitled to work in this country is a criminal offence. Check passports and visas and don't make assumptions.

This chapter only deals with employing people. You may contract people who are self employed and different considerations arise if that's the case.

Even if you only employ one person, it is well worthwhile putting in place the proper documents and policies. It can save on time and money in the long run.

Every employee is entitled to a Statement of Terms which sets out the basic information about their employment. This must be provided to the employee within two months of their start date and must include the following:

- Name of employer and employee
- Date employment began
- Date continuous employment began (taking into account any employment with a previous employer which counts – this will be very rare with a brand new business)
- Rate of pay
- When the employee will be paid e.g. weekly, monthly etc
- Hours of work
- Holiday entitlement including public holidays and holiday pay. Every employee, no matter how long they have been employed by you, is entitled to a minimum of 20 days holiday per year – pro rata for part timers.
- Any provisions for sick pay. You do not have to pay contractual sick pay although many employees will be entitled to Statutory Sick Pay
- Any provisions for pensions
- Notice period
- Job Title and/or brief job description
- If the employment is temporary, the date it is expected to end
- Place(s) of work
- Any details of agreements with Trades Unions (this will rarely apply to new businesses)
- If the employee is going to work abroad for more than one month, details of currency of pay, additional benefits and terms for when they return to the UK.

- Whether there is a contracting out certificate. This will be an issue where you have certain occupational pension schemes. Again, this will rarely apply.

- Details of disciplinary rules and grievance procedures or referring to separate documents where these are contained. You must make sure that these procedures comply with the law and it is worth taking advice on these as failure to follow them can lead to costly Tribunal proceedings.

However, you might want to give your employees a proper contract. This provides much more scope for putting in additional information such as preventing your employees from working for your competitors or giving away confidential information. It must also include all the points above.

Definition

Statutory Sick Pay:

An earnings replacement for employees who are off work through illness. This is paid by the Government.

Handy Tips

Useful websites:

www. businesslink. co.uk

www. hmrc.gov.uk

There are lots of rules and regulations in employment law, so it is always best to check before taking disciplinary action against an employee, changing the terms of their employment or dismissing them.

It is worthwhile having a Staff Handbook containing, as a bare minimum, the following policies:

- Disciplinary and Grievance Procedures
- Equal Opportunities Policy
- Anti Bullying and Harassment Policy
- Health and Safety Policy

You will also need to make sure that you register with Her Majesty's Revenue and Customs as an employer so that they can guide you through the process of tax and National Insurance for your employees.

Employees do have a great deal of rights against an employer. Some of these rights take effect even before the employee is recruited, others start on the first day of their employment and others do not take effect until they have been employed for 1 or 2 years.

Some of the key employee rights are:

- Not to be discriminated against on the grounds of:

  - Age
  - Colour, ethnic or national origin or race
  - Disability (which covers some specific illnesses and conditions, together with long term illness)
  - Pregnancy
  - Sex or Marital Status
  - Sexual Orientation
  - Religion or Belief

- Not to be unfairly dismissed

- If dismissed for redundancy reasons, a right to a redundancy payment after two years' continuous employment

Discrimination can happen unintentionally so, as a general rule, employees should be treated equally regardless of any of the above factors and whether they are employed permanently or temporarily, full or part-time.

There are also important considerations for employees with children under the age of 6 or who are carers, such as the right to request flexible working. Don't worry – there is no automatic right to be able to work flexible hours. Again, if these issues arise, it is well worth getting specialist advice which will save you money and headaches in the long run.

Although reading and following these rules might seem tedious and sometimes an unfair burden it is worth getting them right. Although you can't always prevent disgruntled employees from trotting off to the Tribunal on a whim, making sure you have complied with these procedures will ensure that you have the necessary armor to fight off any claims.

You will also find that ensuring everyone is treated fairly and provided with all relevant information will make for a happier and more loyal workforce.

WRITING YOUR BUSINESS PLAN

'be realistic
with your
goals'

A typical entrepreneur is full of ideas. If this accurately describes you, make sure that you always take a good note of what your ideas are so that they are not forgotten. However, that is not to encourage you to try to run with all of them! A good entrepreneur knows their limitations and therefore knows not to 'bite off more than they can chew'.

All businesses, whether they are a new start-up or a business that has been established for hundreds of years, need a business plan. In brief, this is a document that clearly sets out what the business is, what its aims are for a particular time period and how it is going to achieve those aims.

So why do you need a business plan? Why not just have all of this information in your head? There is more than one answer to this, as follows:

1. It is easier to build a successful business as a team. If therefore one person has dreamed up the aims and aspirations of the company in their head how will others know what these aims are?

2. The bank will want to see the business plan so that they can satisfy themselves in relation to what you are trying to achieve.

3. Any investors will want to see your business plan

4. At the end of each year you can use the business plan to measure how well the business has done in achieving its aims.

Business Plans obviously vary in content and complexity. This book has been written with a 'start-up' company in mind so from here I am going to talk about business plans in the context of a 'start-up', as opposed to an established business.

As I have already mentioned, you are going to use your business plan to document your ideas for the business, communicate those ideas to other people in your team and to show the bank when opening a bank account and applying for finance. Most of the steps that you will go through in this book will go into the business plan. Accordingly, I suggest a business plan structure as follows:

1. Background

1.1 What is the business?
1.2 Why have you chosen this particular business area?
1.3 What is your market? How big is the market?

2. Management Team

2.1 List those who will be involved in the running of the business detailing the following:

- Name
- Previous experience
- Qualifications
- What the person will actually do in the business.

2.2 The 'Management Team' section should clearly show who will look after each part of the business (i.e.: who will ultimately be in charge, who will look after financial matters, who will look after sales etc.). That having been said, do not worry if you are to be a 'one man band' initially. This is very common for a start-up business.

Sample Management Team pages:

More than one person:

i)   **John Smith – Managing Director**

John has spent the previous 10 years as a senior manager
of Dynamic Limited, an automotive company. During this
time he has gained a wealth of experience in running
a company, leading a team of people and in selling into the
automotive sector generally.

John has a degree in Engineering. With his wealth of
experience he will be the Managing Director of the Company.

ii)   **Mike Sharpe – Finance Director**

Mike has spent the last 5 years in the accounts department
of Systems Limited. During this time he has gained a great
deal of experience in all accounting matters.

Mike will be the Finance Director of the Company.

iii)   **Steve Chappel – Sales Director**

Steve has spent the past 6 years as a sales representative
at Dynamic Limited. During this time he has gained valuable
experience in the automotive sector and has experience of
running a sales team.

Steve will be the Sales Director of the Company.

'One man band':

i) **John Smith**

John has spent the previous 10 years as a senior manager of Dynamic Limited, an automotive company. During this time, he has gained a wealth of experience in running a company, leading a team of people and in selling into the automotive sector generally.

John has a degree in engineering. With his wealth of experience, he will initially deal with sales and the running of the Company generally. Once sales reach a certain point, a Sales Representative will be recruited.

ii) **ADD YOUR WIFE/HUSBAND/PARTNER'S name here.** I am sure that they will at least be helping you with admin tasks?

iii) **Unless you are an accountant you will need some accountancy help.** There are many accountants/bookkeepers who freelance by the hour. I would recommend that you seek the help of such a person perhaps just for 1 hour per week. They will record all of your accountancy transactions (i.e.: what you have spent and what you have received from sales). Once you have found someone, put their details here so that the bank knows that someone is looking after this important area of the business.

2.3 When your bank or a potential investor looks at the Management Section, they need to feel that the management team is capable of running the business. That is to say that the team, whether it be one or more people, has the relevant experience and ability to run the business.

2.4 Be aware that whilst a bank or investor may be concerned if the management team looks too small, they can equally be concerned if it looks too big. After all you are a start-up business which is still to prove itself. You do not therefore want to over burden the business with staff costs.

3. Competition

3.1 Who is your competition?

3.2 What will make you better than the competition?

4. Marketing

4.1 What marketing will you do to launch the business?

4.2 How will you attract sales?

5. 12 Month Plan

5.1 What do you want to achieve in the first 12 months?

5.2 How will you achieve the above?

6. Long-term Plan

6.1 What are your long-term plans for the business?

6.2 Where will the business be in 5 years time?

7. Financials

7.1 How much is needed to start the business? (Remember the exercise in Chapter 4)

7.2 How much does the business need for 'Cash Flow' in the first 12 months?

7.3. How much money is the management team investing (if any)?

7.4. How much money is needed from the bank (if any)?

8. Appendix

You should attach the following to the Business Plan;

1. A cash flow forecast (see Chapter 11)
2. A profit and loss forecast (see Chapter 11)
3. Any data that you have referred to in the body of the Business Plan

Finally, make sure that the actual Business Plan itself looks professional. This means make sure that it is typed, not written and that it is nicely bound. In life, first impressions count and if a bank or potential investor sees a handwritten business plan on a scrap piece of paper they immediately will not take you seriously. Don't take my word for it, look overleaf. Which plan looks better?

a) nicely presented plan
b) plan on scrap paper hand written

If you decided that Business Plan (b) looks the best give up now and go back to work!!!

*'your
working
environment
is key'*

YOUR OFFICES / TRADING PREMISES

For the start of this chapter I am going to assume that your business does not trade from its premises (i.e.: it is not a shop etc).

Home Office

When you first start your business you will obviously need to keep your overheads as low as possible, especially whilst you are trying to gain your first valuable sales.

With this being the case, you will need to consider what you really need to spend money on and what you can categorise as being 'luxuries'. Accordingly, unless you need your premises to trade from

this is obviously an area where you can save money initially. For this reason many 'start-up' companies begin life in a spare room at home.

There are only 2 reasons for not setting up office at home, namely; 1) if you need customers to visit your offices (this would not look professional and may put them off) and 2) space. If neither of the above applies, I would recommend that you do start up at home initially. Don't worry about what a bank or potential investor will think. The reality is that they will take comfort from the fact that you know how to economise!

If however you are going to work from home, it is important that you at least have the right equipment. See chapter 4.

If working from home is not practical you will have the following options:

Serviced Office

There are many serviced office providers. A serviced office is an office space that you can rent where everything is included. That means that for one rental payment per month you receive office space, a desk, telephone and computer points. This will be housed within a building with a staffed reception. Accordingly, you will not have to pay any additional payments on top of this, such as rates, heat, light, water etc.

Sounds great? Well the concept is great for a start-up business as it is extremely flexible. Further, most serviced office providers do not require that you commit to any set period of time. This means that you can leave usually on one week's or one month's notice.

However, the obvious drawback is that all of this comes at a premium and the monthly cost is therefore usually fairly high.

Lease

This is where you take out a lease of office space from a landlord, in the same way as you would lease or rent a house. Business leases are typically for 6 months, 12 months or 5 years. This means that you are tied in for this period of time.

Unlike a serviced office, a lease simply gives you office space. It is down to you to find furniture, install telephone lines, install computer points etc. Also, in addition to the monthly rent, you will typically need to pay for business rates and utilities.

Another consideration is that a landlord may not be keen to grant a lease to a start-up business. They may therefore ask for a few months' rent in advance which they will hold as a rent deposit.

Definition

Stamp Duty:

This is the same principle as the Stamp Duty you pay when you buy a house. The only difference is the amount. Click on www.direct. gov.uk for more information.

Handy Tips

Note: *Leases for 5 years or more attract Stamp Duty. This means that you will have to pay Stamp Duty for the lease to be legally binding.*

Purchase

The alternative to the above options is obviously to purchase business premises. Typically you will be able to obtain a 75% commercial mortgage for this. However, the bank will be nervous about granting a start-up business a mortgage and will therefore undoubtedly ask the directors for a personal guarantee. This means that if the company was to default on the mortgage payments that the directors' homes and other assets would come under risk.

A start-up business is always risky. It has no track record and you will not know for some time whether or not it will be successful. With this being the case I would advise that you avoid any long-term commitments on behalf of the business if possible until such time as you are sure that it has a long-term future. It is therefore prudent to either set up at home initially or to agree a short term deal for your premises.

RAISING FINANCE

You have now ascertained your start-up costs chapter 4 and prepared forecasts so that you know how much money you are likely to make and spend and therefore what the flow of your funds will look like (i.e.: your cash flow needs).

Unless you have discovered a business that requires no initial investment and does not cost any money to operate you will therefore have now ascertained how much money you need to raise for your business.

The next step is to make sure that you can raise the required amount. When investigating this add 10% to all of your figures as it is always advisable to 'over-estimate' expenses and under-estimate sales. This will therefore give you an over-estimate of your cash flow needs.

Your main options for raising funds are as follows:

- Own funds
- Bank debt
- Small firms loan guarantee
- Overdraft
- Invoice discounting
- Factoring
- Grants
- Investors

1. Own funds

Potential investors and banks will have far more confidence in you and your business if you have invested your own funds. If you haven't what risks have you taken??

There are a number of different ways of sourcing your own funds:

- Spare cash in the bank
- Sell something
- Re-mortgage your house – i.e.: if you have equity in your house (meaning that the value of your house is greater than the amount of your mortgage) you can approach your current or a new mortgage company and ask them for a bigger mortgage, hence meaning that you will release money from your house
- Obtain a personal loan
- Ask your family and/or friends for a loan

2. Bank Debt

This is simply a loan from the bank for a specified amount. Whilst it is common for banks to loan money to businesses they are always reluctant to do so in the case of a start-up. Further, the bank will always want some form of security for the loan. If your business has no assets (such as stock, a

property etc.) it will not have any security for the loan. The alternative is for the bank to then look to the directors for security. This will be in the form of
a personal guarantee (see Chapter 9).

The other thing that a bank will want to be satisfied about is 'serviceability' of the loan (see Definitions).

3. Small Firms Loan Guarantee

In recognition that many start-up and new companies find it difficult to convince a bank to loan them monies (due to a lack of security), the Department of Trade and Industry (DTI) came up with the Small Firms Loan Guarantee (SFLG). Under this scheme a company can

Definition

Serviceability of the loan:
This means that there is enough cash coming into the business each month to cover the monthly repayment amount to the bank as well as paying the company's other overheads.

obtain a loan under the SFLG scheme if they satisfy certain criteria (see www.sbs.gov.uk). Under the scheme your business receives a loan from a bank. The bank does not ask you for any security as the DTI guarantee's the loan on your behalf. Accordingly, one of the criteria is that you must not have any security to offer. Ask your bank for more details.

4. Overdraft

As with a personal account your bank can agree to allow your business to go 'overdrawn' (that is spend more money than you have in your bank account) up to a specified amount. Whilst this is very quick and easy to set up with the bank the two major drawbacks are that it is an expensive way to borrow money and the bank has the ability at any time to withdraw the overdraft, hence meaning that you would have to repay the

Handy Tips

Whilst nearly all mainstream banks are able to provide a SFLG most do not like doing so. Accordingly, do not expect them to offer this. You will have to ask for it and be persistent when they try to dissuade you.

monies immediately! It is also likely that the bank will ask you for a personal guarantee as security for the overdraft.

5. Grants

It is possible to sometimes obtain a grant from Government authorities, charities or foundations specialising in certain sectors. It is advisable for you to research this.

6. Investors

You could obviously approach a friend, colleague or corporate investor to in effect 'buy into' the business. In simple terms you would give away a percentage of the ownership in your business in exchange for the investor putting cash in.

The obvious disadvantage of this is that you lose some ownership. However, you could hopefully gain another business mind and another person with ideas who also has an interest in the business succeeding. It is also always worth remembering that you are better off having a 'smaller slice of a bigger pie!'

MANAGING YOUR BUSINESS FINANCE

Now we are on to the part of running a business that most entrepreneur's hate, managing finances. Hence the birth of accountants!

We all run finances in our day to day lives, we all therefore have an income and all have expenses/outgoings. However, with a business, finances have to be 'managed' which means that a business must know, on any given day, exactly:

- How much it has received in income
- What the income received was for
- How much it has spent
- What it has spent money on
- How much money it has in the bank
- How much money it currently owes to suppliers
- How much money it is owed
- How much money it is likely to make in the future
- How much money it is likely to spend in the future

From the above a business should be able to produce three important reports, namely;

1. Profit & Loss
2. Cash flow Forecast
3. Balance Sheet

I'm not trying to write an accounts book here so I am keeping this as basic as possible. However, there is a certain level of accountancy understanding that you will need to have to run a business. This will be imperative in making sure that your business survives as well as being important in keeping your bank and any investors confident in your abilities.

Before proceeding any further there are some key words/ phrases that you need to know and understand. These will come up on a regular basis and you need to be able to speak and understand the 'lingo' when talking to banks and investors.

'Profits and Loss'	A summary of how much profit a business has made or how much money it has lost.
'Cash Flow'	A summary monies coming in and going out of a business.
'Headroom'	The amount of monies available to a business after all liabilities have been met in a certain time period.
'Profit'	The excess of revenues over outlays in a given period of time (including depreciation and other non-cash expenses)

'Profit Before Tax'   A company's net profit before deduction of corporation tax.

'Net Profit'   The excess of revenues over outlays in a given period of time (including depreciation and other non-cash expenses)

'Bottom Line'   Same as Net Profit.

'Cash flow Forecast'   An estimate of projected sales, projected cash receipts and projected expense payments that need to be made.

'Profit and Loss Forecast'   An estimate of how much profit a business has made or how much money it has lost.

'Balance Sheet'   A schedule of assets and liabilities of a business

'Break Even'   The point when income equals outgoings.

'Operating Expenses'   Expenses associated with running a business but not considered directly applicable to the current line of goods and services being sold.

'Gross Operating Profit'   Net sales minus the cost of goods or services sold and before payment of taxes and operating expenses.

'Current Assets'   A balance sheet item which equals the sum of cash and cash equivalents, accounts receivable, inventory, marketable

'Current Liabilities'   A balance sheet item which equals the sum of all money owed by a company and due within one year.

1. Profit & Loss

The profit & loss account will tell you how much the business has made (on paper) or lost in a given time period. To compile the report all income and expenditure needs to be listed. For example:

Income:	Sales	£40,000
	Interest received	£1000
Expenditure:	Salaries	£10,000
	PAYE	£2000
	Rent	£2000
	Supplies	£5000
	Electricity	£750
	Heat	£400
	Rates	£1200
	Insurance	£200
	Bad Debts	£270

This information is then put into a Profit & Loss Statement as shown in Example A.

Profit & Loss Statement - 01/01/06 through 01/12/06

Income

Sales			
		Retail Sales	£5,318.00
		Wholesale Sales	£1,567.50
		Consignment Sales	£2,000.00
Total Income			**£8,885.50**

Cost of Sales

	Retail Cost of Sales	£3,419.31
	Wholesale Cost of Sales	£1,001.33
Total Cost of Sales		**£4,420.64**

Gross Profit — **£4,464.86**

Expenses

	Car & Truck Expenses		£100.00
	Freight Paid		£48.95
	Insurance (other than health)		£45.00
	Interest		
		Other Interest	£750.00
	Legal & Professional Services		£178.90
	Lease Expenses		
		Machinery & Equipment	£100.00
		Other Business Property	£12.00
	Supplies		£150.00
	Taxes		£50.00
	Travel, Meals & Entertainment		
		Meals & Entertainment	£1,000.00
	Utilities		£450.00
	Wages Paid		£750.00
	Other Expenses		
Total Expenses			**£3,634.85**

Operating Profit	**£830.01**
Net Profit (Loss)	**£830.01**

2. Cash Flow Forecast

Although profits from a business venture are a measure of success, the flow of cash in and out of a business can be said to be its lifeblood. Cash flow planning is therefore critical to the survival and growth of a business. Unless cash is available at the time it is required, the business may have to close its doors, even though profits are being earned.

The cash flow forecast is an estimate of projected sales, projected cash receipts and projected expense payments that need to be made.

Example B is a typical Cash Flow Forecast layout.

Statement of Cash Flows (£000s omitted)

B

	Year 1	Year 2	Year 3	Year 4	Year 5
Cash Flows From Operating Activities					
Net Income (loss)	(1,454)	(645)	587	3,357	7,901
Add: items not requiring cash in the current period					
Depreciation / Amortization	16	38	66	100	151

B Continued...	Year 1	Year 2	Year 3	Year 4	Year 5
Changes in Operating Assets and Liabilities					
Assets and Liabilities					
Accounts Receivable	(256)	(1,196)	(700)	(3,370)	(5,469)
Inventory	(211)	(698)	(403)	(1,463)	(3,978)
Accounts Payable	114	168	191	526	1,610
Accrued Expense	191	138	174	345	550
Salaries Payable	10	10	11	11	41
Taxes Payable	0	0	0	308	1,009
Reserve for Warranty	24	50	76	183	414
Other Long-Term Assets	(5)	0	0	0	0
Net Cash Provided by (used in) Operating Activities	**(1,571)**	**(2,135)**	**2**	**0**	**2,229**
Cash Flows from Investing Activities					
Capital Expenditures	(64)	(73)	(111)	(182)	(260)
Net Cash Used in Investing Activities	**(64)**	**(73)**	**(111)**	**(182)**	**(260)**
Cash Flows from Financing Equity Investment	2,000	2,500	0	0	0
Net Cash Provided by Financing Activities	**2,000**	**2,500**	**0**	**0**	**0**
Change in Cash	**365**	**295**	**(109)**	**(185)**	**1,969**
Cash, Beginning of Year	0	365	657	548	363
Cash, End of Year	**365**	**657**	**548**	**363**	

This example is an 'annual' cash flow statement. To effectively run your business you would do the same exercise on a monthly basis as well.

3. Balance Sheet

The Balance Sheet sets out your assets and liabilities to show the net worth of your business. Assets owned less liability equal the net worth of your business. By arranging the items in a balance sheet into different groupings, it is possible to understand a great deal about your own business and how it compares to other similar businesses.

The groupings in a balance sheet are as follows:

Handy Tips

Always re-run cash flow forecasts every month.

Current Assets: These are the cash
                                and other assets that are
                                regularly turned into cash
                                or consumed during the
                                normal operating cycle
                                of the business. You use
                                cash to buy materials, sell
                                the products for a gain,
                                and return to cash.

Non Current or Fixed Assets: These are held by
                                the business in order to
                                carry out the revenue
                                earning activities.
                                They are intended
                                primarily for use rather
                                than trading. Examples
                                are: vehicles, plant and
                                machinery as well as the
                                premises that the business
                                operates from.

Current Liabilities: These are amounts owed to outside creditors that have to be met in the ordinary course of business either on demand or within a period not exceeding one year.

Non Current or Deferred Liabilities: These are amounts owed to outside creditors of a relatively long term nature, such as loans

Proprietorship Equity: This is made up of monies put into the business, which is called capital, and the accumulated surplus (or deficit) from the business trading.

Example C is a typical Balance Sheet layout.

Balance Sheet (£000s omitted)

C	Year 1	Year 2	Year 3	Year 4	Year 5
Assets					
Current Assets					
Cash	365	657	548	363	2,332
Accounts Receivable, Net	256	1,452	2,152	5,522	10,991
Inventory	211	909	1,312	2,775	6,753
Total Current Assets	**832**	**3,018**	**4,012**	**8,660**	**20,076**
Property, Plant and Equipment	64	137	248	430	690
Less Accumulated Depreciation	14	50	115	215	324
Net Property, Plant and Equipment	**50**	**87**	**133**	**215**	**324**
Other Long-Term Assets					
Organisation Costs	5	5	5	0	0
Less Accumulated Amortisation	2	4	5	0	0
Total Other Long-Term Assets	**3**	**1**	**0**	**0**	**0**
Total Assets	**885**	**3,106**	**4,145**	**8,875**	**20,400**

Continued...	Year 1	Year 2	Year 3	Year 4	Year 5
Liabilities					
Short-Term Liabilities					
Accounts Payable	114	282	473	999	2,609
Accrued Expense	191	329	503	848	1,398
Salaries Payable	10	20	31	42	83
Taxes Payable	0	0	0	308	1,317
Total Short-Term Liabilities	**315**	**631**	**1,007**	**2,197**	**5,407**
Long-Term Liabilities					
Long-Term Debt	0	0	0	0	0
Reserve for Warranty	24	74	150	333	747
Total Long-Term Liabilities	**24**	**74**	**150**	**333**	**747**
Tax Liabilities	**339**	**705**	**1,157**	**2,530**	**6,154**
Equity					
Common Stock	500	500	500	500	500
Preferred Stock	1,500	4,000	4,000	4,000	4,000
Retained Earnings	(1,454)	(2,009)	(1,512)	1,845	9,746
Total Equity	**546**	**2,401**	**2,988**	**6,345**	**14,246**
Liabilities and Equity	**885**	**3,106**	**4,145**	**8,875**	**20,400**

Ok, so you now understand all about accounts and managing the finance of a business! Don't worry if not, I can tell you that I come across entrepreneurs and Managing Directors of large corporations all of the time who do not understand accounting fully. Just make sure that you understand the lingo and understand why a business needs a profit & loss statement, cash flow forecast and balance sheet. The rest you can leave to your friendly accountant!!

'always look professional'

Your bank will either be your best ally or your biggest business enemy. Obviously you need them to be the former. I cannot stress this enough, even if you think you do not need the bank in the early days it is inevitable that you will need them at some stage.

The first important move that you need to make with regard to your bank is to decide which one to use. Many new entrepreneurs make the classic mistake of 'going with what they know'. This means that they simply use the same bank that they use for their personal banking. In many cases this may work out to be a good idea as inevitably the more business that you give the bank the more valued you will be as a customer. However, this is not always the case. Each bank has its 'good' 'not so good' and 'black' list of business sectors. In addition, each bank has its particular areas where it is particularly strong. For example, some banks specialise in banking law firms which means that they fully understand Solicitor Accounts Rules and other issues that surround solicitor's banking needs. Others do not fully understand Solicitor Accounts Rules as they do not view solicitors as a market that they are strong in.

Accordingly, it is important that you match your business to an appropriate bank which not only has an appetite for your business sector but also has experience in your sector.

Choosing your bank

I would suggest that you follow a 3 step process for choosing your bank as follows:

1. Step One

Draw up a list of banks that

Handy Tips

My granddad used to always say "if you don't ask you don't get". As an entrepreneur starting a new business you need all the favours you can get and, as such, never be afraid to ask for things. The worst that can happen is that you get a no!

both specialise and have an appetite for your sector (these should go hand in hand). To compile this list ask your accountant and solicitor for advice, they should know from their experiences with other clients what the banks are like with different sectors. In addition, you can also ask the banks, although you may not always get the correct answer! If you are still struggling to ascertain this information, send me an email to helpme@deandunham. com as myself and my team have a great deal of experience with many of the banks.

2. Step Two

Compile a list of things that are important to you with regard to your banking needs. These may be as follows:

- **Free banking for a period of time** – remember banks charge for every transaction so every time you bank a cheque, write a cheque, transfer money electronically etc. you are charged. Most banks will give you a 'free banking' period if you ask. Ask for at least one year.

- **Internet banking** – this allows you to control your banking needs online, therefore meaning that can review bank balances and transfer funds. Nearly all banks offer this service but some are better than others.

- **Local branches**
  – this may not be important to you. It really depends whether you want to have the ability to go to a local branch to pay money in. Some banks do not have a great presence on the high street so this should be considered carefully.

- **Loan** – you may have decided that you want to obtain a loan from the bank. See Chapter 10.

- **Overdraft** – you may have decided that you want to obtain an overdraft from the bank. See Chapter 10.

3. Step 3

Meet the banks that you have shortlisted and then decide.

Meeting with the Bank

First impressions count. The bank representative when he or she meets with you will make an initial evaluation of you and your business. This will be based on what you look like, how you come across and how prepared you look.

So, by this stage you would have done the following:

- Decided on a business idea
- Decided on a trading style
- Prepared forecasts
- Ascertained your start-up costs
- Written your business plan

Great, you are now ready to see the bank. If you haven't done all of these things, do not see the bank until you have.

The bank will ask you a number of questions, these may be along the following lines:

- Why did you come up with your business idea?
- What experience do you have in the business sector?
- Have you ever run a business before?
- How much will it cost to start your business?
- Are you investing your own money into the business?
- If yes, where is it coming from?
- If no, why not?
- Do you need a bank loan, if yes, how much?
- What competition will you have?
- What are your future plans?

Handy Tips

Banks like to back true entrepreneurs. If they see that you have drive and ambition they will want to be involved with you and your business.

The answers to these kind of questions should simply roll off your tongue. If they don't, you've not planned your business well enough.

Before you go to your meeting make sure you can tick all of the following:

Meeting Checklist

1. You are wearing a suit
2. You have a good clear explanation of your business, why it's a good idea and how you will take it forward
3. You have your forecasts and can easily explain them
4. You know how much you can invest personally (if applicable) and how much you need from the bank (if applicable)
5. If applicable, you can explain why you need a certain amount from the bank
6. You have a copy of your business plan to leave with the bank and it is nicely bound and looks professional
7. You are feeling confident and enthusiastic
8. You have a list of things that you want to ask for (free banking etc.)

SELLING YOUR SERVICE / PRODUCTS

So you have now finalised your idea, fully researched your market, got your branding together, dealt with any staffing issues, decided where you are going to trade from, written your business plan, obtained the support of your bank and have funds readily available to start running your business. Now the hard work begins! To make this all worthwhile you need to now actually start selling your product/service.

There are of course many different types of products and services all of which suit different types of sales approach. I am not going to focus on any particular type of product or service in this chapter but rather take a 'general' approach. You will therefore need to only use this as a 'starting point' for your sales plan.

Your Attitude

It is fundamental that you believe in the product or service that you are selling. If you do not believe in it this will show when you are communicating with customers and it will therefore follow that your sales will be affected.

If you are going to be selling direct (either yourself or via a sales representative) make sure that you or the representative have a pre-planned well rehearsed pitch.

Know what you are selling

Whether it is a product or a service it is vitally important to know exactly what you are selling. If it is a product, know exactly what it does, what it doesn't do, what its made of etc. If you are selling a service, explain what is included, what is not included etc.

You also need to make sure that you are consistent with what you say about your product or service and with what you communicate in marketing materials.

What are your USP's?

You should know what your unique selling points are. These are the things that are 'unique' to your product or service (that is, things that your competition do not offer). It therefore follows that these are the points that you should be singing from the rooftops!

Who can help you sell?

As well as knowing who your competition is, it is also important to know whom your allies are. Does your product or service go hand in hand with someone else's product or service (i.e. do they complement each other)?

For example:

Dell make computers. However, they do not make the software that is used on the computer, so they team up with companies like Microsoft. Both companies then benefit from the combined package.

My law firm is another example. We do not provide probate services. We therefore have a relationship with another law firm who do so. If we have a client who needs a probate lawyer, we refer them to the other firm. Likewise, if they have a client who is selling their business (which is an area that they do not specialise in) they refer them to us.

This is therefore a great way to attract new business/sales which doesn't cost anything.

Referrers

Consider if there are any individuals or companies who would be willing to refer potential sales to you for commission.

Third Party Sales

Consider if there are any individuals or companies who would want to act as a 'reseller' for you. This means that you sell to them at a 'discounted' price and they then sell on.

There are many different channels for selling your product or service. I would suggest that you prepare a spider diagram of the different options. Also, do not forget to look at how your competition sells their products or services.

I hope that this book has both helped and inspired you.

Establishing and operating a successful business is a really rewarding experience and is therefore well worth the hard work.

Good luck.